12/10

Hanukkah

M. C. Hall

Little World Holidays and Celebrations

www.rourkepublishing.com

www.rourkepublishing.com

Photo credits: Sean Locke/iStockphoto Images, cover, 13; Lisa F. Young/iStockphoto Images, 1, 12; Noam Armonn/ Shutterstock Images, 3; iStockphoto, 4; Nancy Louie/iStockphoto, 5; Rudolf Tepfenhart/Shutterstock Images, 6; North Wind Picture Archives/AP Images, 7; Courtesy of David A. Bernat, 8; Monika Lewandowska/iStockphoto Images, 9; Mike Cherim/iStockphoto Images, 10, 11; Sean Locke/iStockphoto Images, 13; Shutterstock Images, 14; Jose Luis Magana/AP Images, 15; Renee C. Byer/AP Images, 16; Alon Othnay/Shutterstock Images, 17; Lauri Patterson/iStockphoto Images, 18; Sandra O'Claire/iStockphoto Images, 19; Laura Eisenberg/iStockphoto, 20; Howard Sandler/Fotolia, 21

Editor: Holly Saari

Cover and page design: Kazuko Collins

Content Consultant: David A. Bernat, PhD, Assistant Professor of Bible at Hebrew College, Newton, Massachusetts, and Jewish Chaplain at Wellesley College, Wellesley, Massachusetts

Library of Congress Cataloging-in-Publication Data

Hall, Margaret, 1947-
 Hanukkah / M.C. Hall.
    p. cm. -- (Little world holidays and celebrations)
 Includes bibliographical references and index.
 ISBN 978-1-61590-242-2 (hard cover) (alk. paper)
 ISBN 978-1-61590-482-2 (soft cover)
 1. Hanukkah--Juvenile literature. I. Title.
 BM695.H3.H356 2011
 296.4'35--dc22
                                2010009916

Rourke Publishing
Printed in the United States of America, North Mankato, Minnesota
033010
033010LP

www.rourkepublishing.com - rourke@rourkepublishing.com
Post Office Box 643328 Vero Beach, Florida 32964

What are these people doing?

They are celebrating Hanukkah! Jews around the world celebrate this holiday.

Jews are people who practice the **religion** of Judaism.

More than 2,000 years ago Jews in the city of Jerusalem had a beautiful **temple**. They worshipped there in peace.

King Antiochus IV

Then a king from Greece and his army took over the land and the Jews' temple. They put out the oil lamp that was always burning inside the temple.

People still visit ancient Jerusalem.

Some Jews fought back. A family called the Maccabees led them. After three years, the Jews won. They took back the temple.

The Jews wanted to dedicate the temple. They needed to relight the oil lamp. They only found enough oil for one day. But the oil burned for eight days.

Since then, Jews remember this **miracle** during Hanukkah. In **Hebrew**, Hanukkah means dedication. Jews celebrate the holiday for eight days.

During Hanukkah Jews light a **menorah**.
On the first night they light one candle. They say
a prayer when they light it.

Each night after that they light one more candle.
By the eighth night all the candles on the
menorah are burning.

For this reason Hanukkah is also called the Festival of Lights.

Hanukkah is celebrated at the start of winter during the Hebrew month of Kislev.

Many cities put up large outdoor menorahs. People come to watch the lighting of the candles.

People share stories about the first Hanukkah.
They sing songs too.

Children play the **dreidel** game. A dreidel is like a top. Each side of the dreidel has a Hebrew letter on it. The letters give directions for the game.

Families share special meals each night during Hanukkah. They eat foods cooked in oil such as jelly doughnuts and potato pancakes called latkes.

These foods help Jews remember the oil that burned in the temple.

Many families give gifts during Hanukkah. Some children get a gift each night of the holiday. Children also receive money or chocolate coins.

Hanukkah is a very special holiday for Jews.

Craft: Menorah Picture

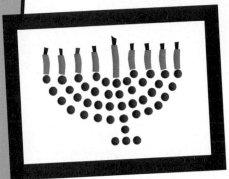

What you need:
- Dry straight macaroni
- Dry lentils
- Red crepe paper
- Glue
- Construction paper

1. Roll little pieces of crepe paper and tuck them into nine straight macaroni noodles so the red shows on top.

2. Each noodle will be one candle in the menorah. Use two noodles together to create the taller middle candle. Glue the macaroni flat onto the construction paper.

3. Glue the lentils onto the paper under the macaroni to form the holder of the menorah. Start at one of the candles on the outside edge. Make a curving line of lentils from this candle to the outside edge candle on the other side. Make three more curved lines of lentils that go from one candle to another. An upside-down T-shape of lentils goes underneath the middle candle.

4. Hang up your menorah picture so your family can see!

Glossary

dreidel (DRAY-dul): a toy marked with Hebrew letters that is spun like a top during a game; the letters stand for Hebrew words that say "A great miracle happened there."

Hebrew (HEE-broo): the language of the Jewish people

menorah (muh-NOR-uh): oil lamp or candleholder for seven, eight, or nine candles that is used in Jewish worship

miracle (MIHR-uh-kuhl): an event that shows God in human life

religion (ri-LIJ-uhn): a system of belief, faith, and worship of God or gods

temple (TEM-puhl): a building where people pray and practice their religions

Websites to Visit

www.chabad.org/kids/article_cdo/aid/358959/jewish/Chanukah-Guide.htm

www.judaism.about.com/od/chanukah/a/hanukkahkids.htm

www.primarygames.com/holidays/hanukkah/games.htm

About the Author

M. C. Hall is a former elementary school teacher and an education consultant. As a freelance writer, she has authored teacher materials and more than 100 books for young readers. Hall lives and works in southeastern Massachusetts.